Skirt Strategies: 249 Success Tips for Women In Leadership

Katie K. Snapp and Carol M. Wight

KATIE K. SNAPP and CAROL M. WIGHT

DEDICATION

Skirt Strategies is dedicated to all young women emerging in leadership, discovering their powerful voice, especially our daughters Andie, Catrina, Kyndall, Laura, Melanie, Sophie, Staci, and Tatiana.

KATIE K. SNAPP and CAROL M. WIGHT

FOREWARD

The global workplace is full of managers, yet not the old-fashioned sort that dictate orders to underlings. Those of today are managers of intellectual talent. That means we are leaders of people and relationships.

Relationship building is an inherent ability in which women are particularly strong, those strengths are natural – yeah, built-in. At Skirt Strategies we believe that by developing women's natural strengths they will excel in the workplace and be more comfortable taking leadership positions.

Our mission at Skirt Strategies is simply this: to change the face of the nation by helping women recognize, develop and fully utilize their natural female leadership skills.

The latest research shows overwhelmingly that a gender-balanced workplace is more profitable and has more integrity than one that is not balanced, namely a male-dominated one. Unfortunately many talented women drop out of the workforce or pass up leadership positions before adding their number to the headcount. This occurs for various reasons. We believe one of those reasons is that women are not comfortable leading with a man's natural skill set, such as divide and conquer, or command and control. Our research has shown that women's natural leadership skills are valuable in this information age but they aren't encouraged in the workplace … *yet*. We are acting as if we need permission to deploy them. Hogwash.

One way to change this is simple: work with women on an individual basis to hone their leadership skills, uncover mental barriers that hinder their full deployment, and enable them to build a world around them where they may thrive as leaders. Frame a big picture strategy filled with personal beliefs and a feminine style, then couple it with techniques to use now, and practice.

That's the Skirt Strategies way.

INTRODUCTION

When the great leaders relate their personal philosophies about their own road to success, it is often a compelling story filled with lumps of wisdom. Most of us find something we relate to, and something we aspire to as well. We all still prefer those simple beacons directing us to clear messages about life and leadership.

This collection of leadership rules is simple too, but in a different way. It brings together over twenty years of enlightened observations from clients, both men and women. Some they originally heard from me, Katie, and many they taught *to* me. When I express them in a workshop and I repeatedly see nods of recognition of a familiar principle, or a life lesson, I know it is a tenet of truth. I witness their stares back at me, lost in the absorption of just "how true that is." I chose to take those pieces and assemble them into something that women in leadership positions could utilize. I wanted the collection to have a feminine side. You might say I am rooting for the underdog, so I tailored those lessons to my fellow businesswomen.

For the second edition, Carol added a rich insight and a perspective of spirituality that I so appreciate, yet might have otherwise missed. Her additions and edits helped us both realize the power of the female outlook. Many tips extend beyond our business environment. They may be a universal truth with equal validity at the office or at home. Probably something fundamental that our parents taught us.

Skirt Strategies is a different format than most management books. Although I like and appreciate the management books that line the shelves of the big box bookstores, or online sources, I rarely find myself lost in one for more than a brief interval. Call me a bad reader, and slightly prone to A.D.D. But I think it goes beyond that. I think we get lost in complex, detailed models. Though they may be well-researched and somewhat effective, they lure us away from the fundamentals that we should rely upon as stepping stones. They should be used in conjunction with a regular visit to the basics, not a replacement to them.

When I see women in the working world scrambling to find a role model to whom they can relate, I wonder if we are going about it all wrong. Those books I just mentioned – ever notice how many are authored by women? Not many.

The entries in this book are heart-of-the-matter reminders for women leaders, whether experienced or new to supervision. Anyone searching for a grounding of her leadership "flavor" will find some nuggets here. You may find that some entries are simply a nice touch. Others are what you may label as non-negotiables.

You will see most written in the first-person for the purpose of simplicity. They come from both Katie and Carol.

You will also see references to terms like teams, supervisors, customers, and so on. If the terms do not apply to your situation, adapt accordingly. Listen for the underlying meaning and fit it into your world.

Often we draw overarching conclusions about the sexes. As you know, it is easy to do, but also a bit dangerous. You could call it stereotyping. However, we believe that looking for patterns based on gender is helpful and we know there is research that proves a man's and a woman's brain operate differently. We are not assuming men will behave a certain way … no, not a chance, not us. But we can do a little predicting based on our experience. After all, wouldn't you say there are some foreseeable behaviors in the opposite sex? So we call these observations "genderalizations." This is a term we have coined and admit as our own. You heard it here first.

Occasionally an entry in the book may hint upon a contradiction. As an example, we suggest that at one time we need to be direct and firm, while other times obliging and easy. That's okay. Our business world is filled with those contradictions, but how we choose to emphasize one rule over another is a part of personalizing it for yourself and painting the picture of you as a strong female leader.

We hope you can easily pick this book up as a quick reminder to what you want from your journey.

We hope you will use it as a foundation for building upon and advancing your career or a work-life combination in which you thrive.

We hope it becomes a beacon for you, to remind you of the essentials that lead to success, on your terms.

Katie & Carol

P.S. TO THE INTRODUCTION

Here's a note of encouragement for the lifelong learners in the crowd.

We have left you lots of open space between tips. Many of these are simply reminders for you. Use them as a prompt for you to true something up, or to get creative with a new approach.

Breathe deep, soak in ideas, challenge yourself. Use the book for notes. Use the book for journaling. Cross out items you disagree with and change them to a personalized entry for you. Then email us and argue why you think differently! We love it! We also love your feedback and ideas. Share them with us at:

www.SkirtStrategies.com

KATIE K. SNAPP and CAROL M. WIGHT

.

SKIRT STRATEGIES

⌒⌒⌒

> 1. Identify what feminine integrity looks like and live toward leading with it.

So often we ask ourselves, "What do I want to do for a living?"

Instead, ask yourself who you want to be in this world. The answer to this question is much more inspiring and is the beginning of your journey to feminine integrity. Who do I want to be?

2. Grow your credibility. Get certifications when you can.

You are always better off having irrefutable credentials. This won't get you all the way there, but it will help.

Lifelong learning is not just a trite saying. It has to do with your continuous curiosity with life. More women are receiving college degrees than men these days, but don't forget to trust your own innate intelligence and ability to learn anything.

What are some of the things you would like to learn more about? Use the space below to begin your "bucket list" of lifelong learning goals.

3. Avoid gossip. It looks immensely unprofessional.

I hate to say it ladies, but we are often labeled as gossipers. That goes hand-in-hand with passing along hearsay, speculating interpersonal clashes, and thriving on unconfirmed fashion reports.

Now I love a drama as much as the next person, and something about being surprised by *who* did *what* is just downright entertaining, but it comes at a cost. At work it costs us our professionalism and the ethical standards of being a safehouse for employees needing a trusted source to take grievances. Think about that.

Here's a way to handle these situations: if you did not see it, it is hearsay, do not repeat it. And do not use it as a basis for discipline. Substantiate any rumor before acting.

If you *did* see it, that does not give you cause to become the source of its circulation.

4. Volunteer to be a conference speaker. You will be surprised at how it strengthens your business acuity.

5. Be prepared when planning to speak in public. Use someone as a sounding board in a dry run.

6. Join a Toastmasters group. They are designed to help people speak in public.

7. Use a coach or a close friend to get feedback from after a public appearance.

We are each subject matter experts in many areas of our lives. Put your experience in a logical, interesting format and you have a speaking topic.

A formal speaking engagement means you must prepare something. And when you are required to put something into a "package" it forces several beneficial outcomes.

The early payoff is an inventory of what you know that others may find interesting. This will build your confidence, because, believe it or not, we rarely assess this outside of that rare family dinner where Aunt Mary sweetly asks what you do for a livelihood.

That is a good thing – a grasp of what you know and what you can accomplish.

When you find the topic to match the forum, prepare. As you create this content, you are defining your subject for an audience in a way that you do not do in the workplace. Your presentation gives you the opportunity to look at your subject from a different perspective and prepare to defend it.

And the pièce de résistance, the thought-provoking Q&A that you may get from an audience. You will gain ideas and subtle areas to extend into for the next speaking engagement.

This is a terrific exercise for you to build confidence and become an expert on your subject matter.

Exercise: Sit down with a pen and paper, and create a list of your lessons learned in _____ (blank). Insert any topic areas, which may include things like:

managing a career and kids
gaining sanity in a day full of mishaps
notes-to-self that I created for being a great leader
solid strengths for someone to have in a high stress job
and so on.

People love lists. They give structure for delivering verbally.

8. Set an example of always being punctual to meetings, as well as starting and ending *your* meetings on time.

Your goal in life – make people's time count. Get there on time. It is a sign of respect as well as efficient time-management.

An observation about your start and end times. Have you ever noticed that when a meeting perpetually begins late, it becomes a meeting that rewards latecomers. And you know the rest of the story …

9. Respect others' time by always having an agenda at meetings.

I have yet to conclude why a lack of an agenda is tolerated. So simple to fix. Perhaps there is a fear of writing a good agenda.

Here is your easy fix for the worst case: Coming to a meeting in which YOU were responsible for the agenda AND you have none. Begin with four statements or questions:

1 – "I want to spend 3 minutes sketching out the roadmap for the meeting today".

2 – "What do we want to walk away with?" A plain way to get to the objectives.

3 – "What major elements will we need to talk about?"

4 – "How much time should that take?"

There will be a strong urge to discuss each topic. Resist. This should only be a discussion about how to map out the topic for agenda-creating, not discuss or problem-solve.

As a footnote, you can use these same four questions to prepare an agenda before your meeting.

Of note, if a rule about requiring an agenda becomes a standard, others will begin showing up and attending meetings more faithfully.

10. Publish something, even if it is a small article in the company newsletter, and include a picture of yourself. It will build your credibility as a leader.

Akin to public speaking, writing forces a thought process that galvanizes your expertise and molds your opinions into text.

For those of you who are good at writing or see yourself as a subject matter expert, challenge yourself a tad more and begin a blog.

An added bonus is your name in print. Your readers associate that with expertise.

11. Don't beat yourself up over something you did. Look forward instead.

Many of us lie awake at night, replaying our own personal bloopers show. Been there. Instead, visualize those thoughts swirling down a toilet. Bye bye. Then replace them with something positive, like a productive outcome.

Try that exercise next time you are in beat-up mode.

12. Remember birthdays and employment anniversaries of the people with whom you work.

13. Be aware of your employees' family life and major events.

Just a card or announcement, but something that indicates that you are on top of it and organized.

Keep extra blank cards in your desk.

14. Don't ever get defensive at work. Even if you have to bury it, don't EVER show it.

Women are more likely to be sensitive to the people issues at work. And when it involves ourselves, the sensitivity heightens. Business issues can be interpreted as personal, and that leads to an increased likelihood of becoming defensive.

When we coach leaders through their challenges, this issue is a tough one. An overblown reaction to any interpersonal dialog immediately puts everyone on eggshells. The potential for success takes a nosedive. Budding partnerships regress.

Think of it this way. At the heart of our defensiveness is some level of insecurity. But instead of working through it in a way that develops it into a growth opportunity, we are throwing chaff out there as a diversion technique and killing the potential for achieving change.

Listen to yourself. Manage yourself. Manage your passion.

15. Stick up for yourself.

A bit opposite of the previous tip but do not let people push you around! Can you do this without getting defensive? You will have to. It takes professional composure and occasionally "sleeping on it" to maintain that composure, but this is critical when building your professional image.

16. Hold people accountable.

This sounds good. Looking for techniques to drive this baby home?

Some ideas. When people have actions that they are supposed to be following up on, implement these techniques:

- Track action items when they emerge, whether you are in a meeting or project discussion.
- Use accountability partners (pairs of action-doers that can use each other for reporting out)
- Broadcast the action items, person responsible, and deadline in various forums, such as minutes or online dashboards. The more visibility, the better.
- Clearly use "sponsor" or other term identifying a single point of contact for an action and have that person's name directly associated with the task.
- Use standing agenda items that review *who* is doing *what*, so that it becomes

expected that the responsible person will be answerable to the group. A standing agenda item is one that is automatically included on an agenda. This forces the topic and people begin to expect a discussion on it.

By the way, the pre-requisite of acting accountable is knowing what is expected of you. That's another topic.

17. Always be clear to your superiors about what you believe your level of authority is.

In other words, have regular conversations about what you believe your boundaries are. You are likely to have more authority than you think. Take advantage of that and you will be seen as a go-getter.

Have a conversation with your boss that may include questions like:

Do you think I take as much initiative as needed?

Is there anything you'd like to see me doing more of?

Are there any times when I can or should be taking more advantage of my level of authority?

18. Use a team meeting to select a local non-profit project and decide on a plan to support it over the next year.

Better yet, let your staff make suggestions for charities they would like to support. Then give them two weeks to lobby on behalf of their project, giving everyone an equal vote as to which non-profit they support for the year.

We have included a community-focus tip here because women are such natural players in the charitable world. We have a high awareness of the importance of community and the greater good.

19. Encourage your employees to give back to the community. Support them.

Formalize your policy on charitable time. Tell staff they can have one hour a week or month to donate to a charity of their choice. Get a letter from the Executive Director of the charity that your employee is in fact donating his or her time.

[insert warm, fuzzy feeling here]

20. Pass up the temptation to quip if it runs the risk of hurting someone's feelings.

21. Never underestimate how far trust can get you.

This is a justification for investing time in developing strong relationships. In a model we use at Skirt Strategies, trust is built upon the interpersonal skill of making and keeping agreements. Seems so simple, but when you consider it, many amiss relationships have originated from a communication misfire. One person meant this – the other heard it that way – someone jumped to a conclusion – a negotiated agreement toppled because of a change. Happens all the time. It can be prevented through ongoing, stringent communication that is open and regular.

Consider a relationship you have where trust is critical. Then assess your level of open and regular communication, where expectations are discussed. Could the interaction be strengthened? Do you need more dialog about each other's expectations?

The Speed of Trust by Stephen Covey is a good reference book for this tip.

22. Establish strong relationships with people at work.

Becoming friends with many people at work allows you insight into them personally. Relationships sprout into areas that would otherwise be stagnate. Some relationships may also help you move up to the next level, or develop alliances between departments.

Willingness to know people at a non-professional level also illustrates your willingness to stretch – a characteristic that will serve you well when needing to relate in politically sensitive situations. This is a feminine characteristic that may be missing in a male-dominated workplace. Make it your business to see this changed. What if *you* were the one reason that someone was looking forward to coming to work?

Be genuine about your curiosity of others. Get to know what makes them come to work every day. Is it their kids, their coin collection, or their need to discuss their wine obsession with someone?

The challenge is to learn something new about your closest circle of workmates.

23. Dress smart and professional. Never sexy.

24. Look styled and well kept: nails, hair, and subtle jewelry.

25. Wear a minimal amount of perfume to work or, better yet, none at all.

26. Dress for the position to which you aspire.

Take advantage of your feminine side? Absolutely.

Go too far and you've become a distraction instead of a pleasant asset to have around. This is a grey area and open to interpretation based on your personal background, what is suitable to you, and the culture of your industry. Heels just a little to high or a skirt just a little too short send a completely different message. Remember, unless you are in an industry where it's all about how you look (like the fashion industry), you'd like to be valued for how you think.

Inappropriate appearance can come at a high cost so err on the side of safe. Check yourself before walking out the door. Bend forward in front of a mirror and see whether you are revealing too much cleavage. We just don't believe that peek-a-boob belongs at work.

If you don't have cleavage, we'll give you something else to do - bend over forward and make sure your skirt is not too short.

27. Learn how to give directions precisely.

Use real directions, like north, east, south, and west, rather than rattling on about landmarks and personal observations.

People don't care about which church your niece got married in or the site of the last place you were seen with your pantyhose caught up in your skirt.

(That's a real story ...)

28. Own personalized stationery. Use the USPS for a kind note to a customer.

If you are in a competitive industry, you know that defining your value proposition is an ongoing exercise. Edging the competition makes a difference and using the old USPS may make that difference.

If you are not in a competitive industry, you should still like this entry, because setting yourself apart is *always* a good idea.

But the special touch of a hand-written message, sent from a person rather than a company, and using the snail mail instead of the electronic mail, says something about your manner. Remember that subtle level of excitement as a kid when you received a letter in the mail? Nice.

A challenge: pick 3-5 people that you'd like to thank for anything and show your gratitude with a quick note. Don't overthink it. Just a simple thought and drop it in the mail.

Gratitude is like karma; it comes back to you in unexpected ways.

29. Share your garden vegetables with your co-workers.

My dear uncle, living in New York City, read this one and stated wryly, "I have *no* idea what you mean by this." I had to laugh. If you live in an urban area where home gardeners are a rarity, consider this one metaphorically. Or substitute "homemade cookies" for "garden vegetables."

30. Keep leadership and teambuilding books on your shelf, including inspiring books on CD. Use the good ones as reference when you need ideas.

If you enjoy listening to audio books or podcasts, there is a pleasant byproduct to this tip. Instead of the news or TV, opt to listen to something on your iPod. You'll be surprised at how much of the negative clutter you eliminate from your life. Positive internal messages result.

If the last audio device you used was called a Walkman, then you are rapidly becoming a dinosaur. Getting into the 21st century is critical to your image at being adept and on the forefront. I don't care if you don't know how. Learn. Ask the nearest teenager to teach you. Gotta get with it, babe.

31. Encourage your employees to check out any of your books.

You are responsible for creating the environment where others should thrive. When you design your surroundings around what you value, it permeates to those that live there.

Consider how knowledge and intellectual growth will contribute to performance and how it will make the work environment a place of learning.

32. Keep a book of trivia in your office. It makes you look interesting.

Banter with your employees over interesting trivia.

There will always be something interesting in a trivia book, regardless of the background of your employees. Use that as a wedge into the conversation at the lunch table, or build the reputation of those books so that they become references in the workplace conversations.

If you'd like ideas for which books to get, take a minute to wander around a bookstore. It's always enjoyable to see what quirky subject-matter someone is writing about that may enthuse your friends.

This is also an excellent exercise for building the brain and using what has been recently discovered as neurogenesis. We actually build new brain cells through mental challenges like discussing trivia,

That's right! You can recover those college party years of brain-cell killing.

33. Tough conversations are easy to avoid. Have the courage to make them happen.

The "dreaded conversation" takes guts and the discomfort is usually worth the outcome. To make it happen effectively takes some know-how, but not as much as you might think, and if you start out on the right note, the likelihood of success is good.

Work with a coach to get adept at opening up the tough conversation, script the first few lines, or review a conflict management technique to help get started.

Our challenge to you if you are avoiding a particular conversation:

- Begin by writing down how you will initiate the conversation
- The goal you would like to accomplish by having the conversation

The rest you will not be able to script, so woman-up and make the appointment to talk.

The right thing to do is often the most difficult thing to do.

34. Do not hesitate to forgive. But don't be a pushover either.

Remember that forgiveness is for you, not necessarily for the other person. It is for your heart to let go of any resentment.

We may have a tendency to hold on to something if we think wrong has been done, but you may want to think about what that does to inhibit your forward development.

35. Hum or whistle, but don't skip.

36. Get to the point by using efficiency in your language.

We are not going to expand upon this.

37. Know when not to be too blunt. Know when to be a little blunt.

38. Respect the support personnel.

Who are the unsung heroes that make your business "work"? Departments that run back room activities rarely get to interact with the external customer and are often forgotten as a key cog in the productivity wheel, yet you could not function without them. The glory goes to those with the authority and visibility, and it sometimes creates a sense of unimportance to those that work to help others shine. Those employees that make it all come together in the background are easily forgotten, like the stage crew in a fabulous show.

Examples - the administrative staff, the HR department, the warehouse, IT, printing & publications, accounting.

Promote the importance of the support personnel by listening to their needs and expectations. Acknowledge them with earned praise. They may not get it elsewhere.

Is there someone right now that you can think of to recognize with some positive feedback?

39. Keep track of anything you borrow and return it in a timely fashion.

40. Buy whatever your employees' kids are selling.

41. Participate in the blood drive.

42. Be a lifelong learner.

Skirt Strategies has an essential teaching model that includes ongoing growth. As women, we have a high-awareness of our potential and are constantly facing challenges to personal development. Because of that, we engage more frequently in classes, workshops, and reading self-help.

We love the fact that women are experiential learners and that we reach out to networks that promote self-development.

43. Pass your skills on to others. Teach a class.

Even more important than speaking in front of an audience, teaching hones your expertise on a subject. It also symbolizes your priority to give back to others.

44. Do not accept the notion that some people will never change. It's not your call.

As soon as you decide to give up on someone, all else is bleak. Especially for that person.

This is more of a message to you about how you *approach* those that may look unpromising rather than accepting the fact that all people can change. Do not expect monumental growth in everyone, but don't toss him to the wolves if you do not see potential. There may be situational factors that hold him back. There may be deeply-seeded barriers to productivity of which you are unaware.

Perhaps you make a pact with yourself that you give a person three attempts at redirection before you make a more drastic move.

At some point, there will be individuals that do not fit on your team. Some will take invested time and energy to develop, without any guaranteed outcome. If you choose not to make that investment, simply acknowledge that he belongs somewhere else. Do not conclude that he will never change.

That's not your call.

45. Identify a role model to aspire to. If it is a man, identify what he would look like as a successful female leader and adopt those characteristics that impress you.

Often the easiest way to see through a situation is to ask yourself what your role model would do.

Here's an example: Let's say you are getting some pushback from an employee. You have asked him to deal with a certain situation and he has stated that he really does not want to. Your gut tells you he is the most appropriate and capable person for this assignment, and it creates other dilemmas if he does not take it. Yet he is acting like he can make the call.

Now consider your role model for effective leadership, and how she would handle the situation. Perhaps she would allow the employee to state his concerns, then she would stick with her original decision, and firmly state how it would be. Gentle confrontation.

Replicate what your role model would do. Your voice, and your words. But with the same intent and objective as your role model.

46. Remember, your business is about people, regardless of your product or service.

You are probably better at "people" management than most men.

The old standard about a person's competency being measured by IQ is rapidly being debunked. We now know that EQ, the emotional parallel, is more important for leadership and effectiveness in general. EQ stands for Emotional Quotient and is often called emotional intelligence. It mostly refers to how aware you are of yourself, your emotional response to the world around you, as well as sensing emotional posture in others.

In the information age, we are dependent on interaction with people, their intellect and our relationship with them, not assembly lines full of widgets. Women are more adept at most of the areas of emotional intelligence than men and research is telling us that our sensing abilities and insights are invaluable to company cultures, as well as bottom line health.

Appreciate yourself for these inherent aptitudes.

47. Do not expect something for nothing. Instant gratification is a curse of our society.

48. Fix things without a fight

When people are upset about something, they may have prepared for a fight. It sets them off guard when you apologize. And if she is a customer, you may even want to admit fault, even if it's not your fault. You'll never "win" a fight with a customer. As Oprah states, "I would rather have *peace*, than to be *right*."

It takes the wind out of their argument when you apologize and turns the conversation to problem-solving rather than venting and blaming. This is something women do well.

49. Keep your customers happy by saving them effort.

A little trick in testing your customer service. It is in the form of a question:

Is the customer having to put forth an effort to get service?

If the customer is overextending to interact with you, then you are not adequately serving her. Are you asking her to call back and ask for someone else, or are you taking her number and seeing that you are the one that follows up? Are you forcing her to figure out the system to find her answers, or are you moving toward her to discover her needs? That's the difference.

50. Know your customers and where you stand with them.

It's easy to get lost in the process, forgetting to maintain a level of superior customer service. Occasionally step back and check the relationship.

The most important question to include on a survey of customer satisfaction is "Would you recommend us to a friend?"

51. Spend a little time each day wandering among your employees.

52. Judge your workplace by the number of smiles and degree of laughter.

53. Always show pleasure at the success of others.

Find a fun, creative and tangible way to recognize employees for a job well-done. Even gold stars – yes like the ones you got in 2nd Grade – make people feel good about an accomplishment.

Think this is silly? Just wait until you see them compete over who has more stars.

54. Fit in, but do not become one of the boys.

There is a line that a woman should never cross. Once you do, your feminine individualism goes adrift. I am talking about women that feel they must act like a man to be accepted as a leader.

Relate to men? Yes. Understand men? Yes. Conform? Hmm, depends on how you define that.

You are undeniably you, and that includes being female, including the assets and liabilities that accompany the gender. Burying those qualities is robbing others of the opportunity to appreciate them. Stick to your guns.

55. Strive to be more articulate in your communications. Successful women leaders are usually very eloquent.

Public speaking may be a prevalent fear among the general population, but leaders must decide early in a career to build it into an asset. The last time I heard a leader fumble through an off-the-cuff speech, I moaned internally at what it must be like to hear him in a meeting. Following that, I noted my impression of his capabilities had just descended a notch. That's what is at stake here.

My colleague Matt Rix has a presentation he titles "You Ain't No Leader If'n You Caint Talk Good." You may be great at your job, but if you do not come off polished ... *baaaad.*

Good thing for the public speaking associations and top-notch training classes that give you the experience, because that is the best way to overcome poor speechmanship.

Practice it, present it, and ask for feedback.
Lather, rinse, repeat.

56. Say "hello" first to others in passing.

Look people in the eye when greeting others and ask your staff to do the same.

57. Keep a spare umbrella at work for someone in need.

58. Say "Thank You" when passing the janitorial staff in the hall.

You may even add a comment about how great the office is when it is clean.

Test this one out on a city employee working somewhere in public, like picking up litter in the park or sweeping a sidewalk. The typical response – complete shock because they have clearly not received adequate positive feedback.

59. Surprise your employees with unexpected treats, preferably brain food and not doughnuts.

IF you decide to indulge, make it worth the calories. A homemade cake from a coveted recipe is distinctive. Offer something special, after all, people EXPECT women to be able to cook. (wink wink) They LOVE that about us!

So let's say you don't bake, you are certainly capable of picking out great pastries. Remember, boxed brownies are almost as good as homemade.

60. Have a small area rug and a warm table lamp in your office. It will make the room more comforting.

61. Keep a plant or flowers on your desk.

62. Ask the facilities folks if you can paint your office. (Don't choose pink – just my bias.)

I am a huge fan of comfortable environments. Why make your workplace cold? Did it ever occur to you that you could do a little decorating?

If you have enough natural lighting and a table lamp, you can extinguish the fluorescent. Really – this makes a huge difference.

63. Commit your department to continuous
improvement.

When your department does something well,
learn from it so that you can replicate it in the
future.

Want to differentiate your leadership capabilities
from others? Become process-focused. That is,
look at everything as a system that is designed
and operating as intended, then it repeats itself.

Becoming process-focused can envelop you and
can become a vast effort. Without getting
overwhelmed by that, consider the baby steps
that are involved and see some immediate payoff
in productivity and decreased errors.

To do this, take these basic steps.

1. Identify what critical activities your
   department performs.

2. List those activities in sequential steps, with
   a beginning and an ending.

3. Name each as a process (give it a label).

KATIE K. SNAPP and CAROL M. WIGHT

4. Create a "**T**" chart with two areas of discussion – what is working, and what is not, one on each side of the "**T**". Use this chart as a basis for getting employees involved. Problem solve. Track improvements. Reward wins. Feel the progress!

As you become more comfortable looking at your business area as a process, you can stretch by adding more activities.

For those of you that are advanced in process improvement, consider your critical processes and list them. Generally, they will evolve and change on their own over period of time, and need a re-look about every 12 months.

64. Always accept a compliment graciously.

65. Laugh at yourself when you screw up. Humor is an anti-depressant.

66. Be an example at your workplace for both men and women by setting the standard for honor and equity.

When someone else plays dirty, it should never be an excuse for you to lower your standards. Instead, see it as an opportunity to show your resoluteness for upholding the truth and doing the right thing.

67. Know when to ask for more time before making a commitment.

68. Know when to be decisive.

A common weakness for women is decisiveness. Sometimes our effective approach of bringing others into a decision is interpreted as waffling or insecurity in making a decision. This is an area where many of us could grow.

Sometimes there is no clear choice between A and B. This is the time to muster all of your feminine qualities, including intuition, and just make a decision based on what you know at the time, even if it feels a little risky. Some of your justification may come from gut-feelings – listen to this intuition.

Don't be afraid to decide. It's not life or death. Just a decision. Unless, of course, it is life or death, then ignore this completely.

69. Don't take any message as gospel until you have heard it from the source.

Remember that "telephone" game in grade school?

Messed-up messages are common, frequently unintentional, and dangerous. Not checking your sources can be perilous to your credibility and will eventually affect your professionalism.

Stay away from gossip too.

70. Profile your team for personality styles so that they can appreciate and understand one another by styles and not by gender.

High-performing teams have characteristics that can be replicated. One of them is an understanding of the individuality of each member beyond his or her gender, race, or age.

An additional benefit of this effort is a diffusion of gender-blaming. When people learn styles, they are less likely to label a behavior as something "that a girl does". Instead they learn that it is the person's behavioral trait, not a gender-trait.

Relationship-building based on style creates extremely strong interactions and a high potential of success. Yes, it takes more work, but remember your commitment to continuous improvement.

71. Shake hands firmly, make eye-contact, but send a soft message with your eyes. Project a warm, welcoming image.

The days of the shrinking violet are over. No one likes a limp handshake. It makes you feel dirty, as if you just touched a wet fish.

72. Soften up. Be authentic. Be you.

Appreciate the valuable qualities you bring to the workplace.

Here are our 16 feminine leadership traits from the Intuition Model. Select ONE and watch yourself doing it over the next week.

Collaborative mindset	Inspiring
Mediating relationships	Building
Planning	Multi-tasking
Social equity	Involving others
Keeping perspective	Interpreting
Sensing undercurrents	Empathizing
Sensing intent	Listening
Emotional intelligence	Big picture thinking

73. Don't let conflict go unresolved.

Occasionally a conflict evaporates after a time, but letting that happen is risky – it's that ol' "procrastination pays" philosophy.

"We affect change by engaging in robust conversations with ourselves and others."

- Fierce Conversations by Susan Scott

Change will not happen in your business world unless you are willing to face some difficult conversations, and that may take courage.

This might be a good tip topic for taking an action on ...

74. Ride your bike to work once a week or more.

75. Give away bus passes to encourage others to save gas.

Simply thinking green.

Let your workforce drive this effort. Start an Alternative Transportation Committee to facilitate other travel methods and educate the employees about options.

76. Soak up the sun for five minutes a day. It will help your complexion and make you feel better.

There are many proven benefits of Vitamin D, including an increased immune system, as well as lowering risks of some cancers. Don't turn a few minutes in the sun into dangerous exposure though.

Simply enjoy the outdoors, smile at the center of the solar system, and let your face be warmed. It will be reflected in your complexion and attitude.

77. Schedule time in your day for yourself.
    Enjoy it quietly.

Every day needs to include time for you, if only 10 minutes.

This is a challenge for those of us with kids and work and home. Even if the time alone is the drive from daycare to work, turn off the radio and external noise, state your gratitude, and be in joy if only for the moment.

78. Clean up others' messes in the break room, but not too often. (They will think you are their mother)

I worked in an office at one time where a member of the clerical staff had put up a sign stating

Your mother does not work here.
Clean up your mess!

Later someone took the liberty of scribbling his own retort to the rule by adding

Are you sure?
Because that sounds JUST like my mother?

Be helpful, but do not become the motherly figure taking on cleanup patrol. It creates a dependency, just like at home.

79. Show care and attention: look people in the eyes.

The phrase I keep in mind is this: *Listen to Learn.*

Listen deeply to the other person, as if you were going to write a paper on the dialog. When you do that, you will look at them with an attentiveness that illustrates your concern and care.

Every so often repeat what someone says verbatim. "So what I heard you say is ... Is that correct?" This helps you concentrate on listening and lets the other person know that you are interested. Try this with your husband. It is easy and makes him feel special.

80. Be open to new ideas.

81. Do something to make yourself feel better, not to get the recognition.

82. Practice a random act of kindness once a week.

Ideas:

- Pick up someone's mail
- Donate your parking space
- Bring someone coffee
- Leave a $10 gift card to lunch on someone's desk
- Replace someone's tissues with those soft lotion ones

83. Ask your employees for opinions, but always let them know your justification if you do not implement their ideas.

Try to be nice and see what you get! *(heavy sigh)*

Women are adept at being inclusive and soliciting opinions of others. This does not necessarily undermine our authority; in fact it reflects an openness to incorporate others.

Despite your good measures, there will be times it backfires. A common pitfall is asking someone his opinion. Translated, he interprets it as invitation to influence the outcome of a decision.

If you do ask someone for his opinion, be sure to position it. Continue to ask for opinions, but use helpful statements like:

I want your opinion because I am trying to see what the majority position is.

I want your opinion because I am simply looking for ideas.

I want your opinion and it may or may not have an impact on the outcome. I don't know yet.

84. Involve your employees in daily decisions.

In a staff meeting, ask the question "What does success look like?"

This is a kickoff to excellent brainstorming, where there are no wrong answers. Let people get a little crazy in their responses.

Even if you don't have employees, this is a terrific question for visualizing achievement.

85. Regularly review your tasks and see which can be delegated. Others may see it as a growth opportunity and a change of pace.

An easy way to get the employees more bought-in: involve them and delegate to them. When they experience the in's and out's of issues, they engage in a desired outcome.

86. Have a plan for your future and work towards it.

A friend once reminded me "If you can dream it, you can do it."

Use your vision statement to inspire your vision of success. If your vision statement does not inspire you, then use these steps to create one that will.

1. Begin with an understanding of what you believe you are here for. For many women, that is some level of helping others.

2. Decide what success looks like in the future

3. Articulate it by crafting a sentence or two or draw a picture

4. Put it somewhere that looks back at you regularly – maybe your dressing room mirror, your dashboard, or the cookie jar.

Start dreaming. Watch opportunities line up that support your dream.

87. Be known for something unusual, such as reciting the Greek alphabet.

88. Occasionally resist the urge to take over.

89. Don't try to act like a man. (Except for cursing ... see next item).

Ladies, our ball-busting days are over. Men *enjoy* having us in the workplace, as long as we are not trying to act like someone trying to outpower them.

Research has shown that women who act like a man in a leadership position often fail to influence others effectively. Many go down in flames.

We do not have to prove we can out-man the men.

90. If you are prone to cursing, fine. But know who appreciates and understands it and who is offended by it. Be careful.

Actually, I think I wrote this one as a reminder to myself ...

91. Remember that you stand for what you tolerate.

This reminder is one that may need some introspection. Ask yourself several questions about what it may mean to you.

92. Give someone the benefit of the doubt. After that, make him earn your trust.

Too bad … we live in a world where others want to see what they can get away with, and they started in their terrible two's. Imagine! For those people, we are defined by our boundaries and their purpose in life is to test them. Know where you will give and where you will not negotiate. Your maternal instincts will benefit you here.

93. Mentor your employees, not just the women.

94. Keep in mind that the biggest growth in your career probably resulted from a challenge.

Continue challenging yourself. Know that the next big step is possibly that big, fearsome decision that you are avoiding.

95. Remember to pass along your perspective to your employees. You are in a position to see more than they see.

Your unique position as a woman as well as a leader gives you insight. You attend meetings that your employees do not. Decisions that may make sense to you are sometimes illogical to those around you. You speak a different language and run in a different circle, at least occasionally.

What may be second-nature to you could be unfamiliar to those that report to you so err on the side of over-communicating. Teach them what you experience, and pass along your lessons learned.

96. Be absolutely relentless about who you hire. A little extra time filtering to get the right people will greatly pay off later.

Perhaps **the most undervalued procedure** in the workplace is the hiring process. As the potential boss of a new hire, you should be insistent on getting the right people on your team. The ordeal begins with a lucid understanding of what you are looking for in an employee, both technically as well as behaviorally. Co-workers of the prospective employee should have input on this as well. Then a rigorous interviewing process that includes cross-checking what you have discovered.

Groan. Yes, it is effort, and it should be.

Next time you have to justify an increased salary in a job offer to someone new, consider an employee that did not work out and tabulate what THAT costs you.

Use a pre-employment screening service that offers assessments. These personality tests can tell you more about a person than any interview. The service will also recommend how to go forward with the hiring process.

97. Invest in your people like you would in a financial portfolio. You want them to develop, mature, and endure.

98. Be an avid goal-setter and lead your employees through the same process.

99. Reward achievement of goals.

Your budget should account for professional development education, including yourself. These can be linked to personal and professional goals.

100. Keep a wall mirror in your office.

My mom often has an overlooked spot in the back of her head, where hairy little nest of turmoil resides, recluse from her brush. Avoid pillow-head by strategically positioning a second mirror. (Sorry mom)

101. When you need a friend, look at yourself in the mirror and make a monkey face.

Check your appearance for appropriately looking the leader part, as well as an admirable monkey impression. Use a magnifying mirror (don't be scared ...), especially if you require reading glasses, to apply makeup and pluck anything staring back at you.

102. Find a trick to memorizing people's names

103. Be personable when talking to others by casually using his or her name in the conversation.

Your attentiveness to others is crucial. Forgetting a name here and there is not uncommon, but remembering more often than the normal Jane will get you ahead with relative ease.

For starters, being introduced to someone will be your cue. A red flag will begin waving in your head. If you do not hear their name, ask. Listen, study the face, then memorize. What does it rhyme with? Who does he look like? Can I write it down somewhere quickly.

Then put it into play in the conversation by using his or her name and you have sent the message of caring and listening.

104. When contributing to a conversation, self-check that it does not come off as a "one-up."

Starters like "Oh that's nothing ... listen to this..." or "I have a better story" are sure indications that your listeners may see your input as boastful.

Your verbal involvement is especially critical in larger groups where the air-time is limited and can quickly get out-of-hand. Before talking, consider whether what you are saying is indeed a value-added tidbit rather than a need to position yourself as an authority.

Sometimes silence portrays knowledge and wisdom better than having an opinion on every topic.

105. When going by your female intuition, don't feel you have to justify it to your critics.

Don't overuse your hunches, unless, of course, they are never wrong.

Natural instinct is a wonderful tool. It comes from a place of knowledge, experience, and perhaps a deep gut feeling. It is easy to lose your confidence about the intuition if someone questions it as unfounded. Stick with it, girlie.

> **106.** Pick your fights. Do not equate silence with weakness.

Every once in a while stand up for yourself.

Many women are usually very accommodating, not seeing the necessity in stirring the pot. See to it that you occasionally stand up for yourself when your beliefs and your opinions are at stake. Do it in a professional manner, and not in the heat of the moment.

It's refreshing and you may get noticed as a leader.

> **107.** When arguing, always leave room for the other person to keep his dignity.

Whoa there .... count to TEN ....are you jumping to a defensive stance? Check your emotions. Make sure the battle is worth it before you engage.

108. Don't use time or words carelessly. Neither can be retrieved.

A quick wit is a gift. A sharp tongue invokes fear.

A scathing remark should only be used as a last resort, and even then should be followed by a cooperative comment. Statements should never be about *who* a person is. Keep the personal remarks out of it.

Remember that comments like these are likely to be interpreted as you feeling threatened. Now why in the world should you feel threatened by others? You are better than that.

109. Watch your female charm. Use it for good and not evil.

There is no reason a woman cannot have a feminine flair. We cannot escape it and we shouldn't. Be proud of the differences you bring to the workplace.

We bring leadership that feels compassionate, inspirational, empathetic, collaborative, and intelligent. Those are female charms! Y'know the world needs them.

110. Turn a negative condition around by looking for a single benefit.

At the end of your day, list all that you are grateful for.

Then take at least one negative from the day, and turn it around into a gratitude. For example, "I am grateful for that jerk that cut me off in traffic today. He reminded me to come back to being a patient, loving person ... even for idiots like him."

111. Be timely when responding to customers, whether they are internal or external to the company.

Consider a personal policy that you return calls within 24 hours. If possible, have the same for email and other correspondence.

Just do it. Quit picking everything apart. Get to the results.

112. Look to achieve greatness for your group but don't get bogged down in the details.

Starting is the most important step to reaching a goal. They say that women are not decisive (who are *they* anyway?). Let's work together to change that perception. Make the decision to lead greatness. Start now.

113. Don't be intimidated by a man. Pretend he is acting out because he is intimidated by *you*.

114. Don't have a fear of being wrong.

Does anyone really expect *no* mistakes from you? Be fearless, oh great one.

115. Take responsibility for your actions by facing them head-on.

We see examples daily of leaders blaming others for the state of affairs. Aren't we all looking for the leader that will quit the blame-game?

Take responsibility and DO something about it. Be that leader. We are not victims.

116. Being a female leader is like living in New York City – if you can make it there you can make it anywhere. Hang in there.

Here's our recipe for your leadership cocktail:

1 part knowledge
1 part inspiration
1 part responsibility
10 parts moxie

You should always be focused on the goal. Let others be focused on the details. Inspire others to be their best. You *can* make it anywhere. And remember this cocktail when you are anxiously awaiting for happy hour.

117. Do not give the naysayers your prolonged attention. Take account of their position and then blow past them.

Some people submit to the church of negativity. Bad religion. Don't let their beliefs be a part of your subscription. Recognize the limitations and move toward the positive.

118. Leave your job a little better than you found it.

119. Don't compromise your femininity by always wearing suits or dull colors.

Looking the female leader role does not mean looking the masculine role.

I was once in the Crown Room at Atlanta on a layover, dressed in business casual with a vibrantly colored blazer. The man working next to me interrupted me to share how much enjoyed my bright business attire.

Funny how memorable it is when someone pays us a compliment.

This is also a statement about the rapidly changing wardrobe for women. How dull are those suits you are wearing? Watch the national television anchors for ideas. They often look tailored, stylish, and yet still feminine.

120. When in a pinch, ask yourself *what would be the right thing to do?*

This is a quick litmus test that can often flesh out the best path when you are conflicted over a decision. Somewhere in there you know the *right* thing to do.

Asking this simple question often lights the way.

And it keeps your integrity intact.

121. Resist making a decision when you are upset.

Remember, as a woman you may be more hard-wired for emotion and it can affect your clarity.

Brain differences in men and women have been proven. It is okay to be different, and, know what? It is okay to be emotional. Just don't let it get the best of you.

When you do sense the emotion creeping up, the best approach is to call upon your self-management by taking a moment, centering yourself, then make the best decision while keeping your goals in mind.

122. Expend energy as if you have it to throw away.

I love the thought of this ...but it makes me tired. You young people can go do it.

123. Measure people by the size of their hearts, not by their position or authority.

The value of a woman in the workplace is her ability to bring compassion. Treat everyone with respect. You never know how it will be returned, but the law of circulation guarantees it.

124. Stand up straight.

125. Sit up as if you have all the confidence of the CEO, whether you aspire to his position or not.

126. AS IF … those two small words are a secret to a great leadership technique.

Act *as if* you are confident speaking to the group
Act *as if* you know what you are doing
Act *as if* you are in control of the room

Sending the message is as important as truly feeling it. And once you live it long enough, you really will start feeling *as if*.

When a leader exudes confidence, others sense it and begin to put trust into her. This, in turn, builds her conviction and it becomes a self-fulfilling prophecy.

It's a neat little trick that those of us in public speaking like to use quite a bit too.

127. Treat your employees with respect. Remember, when they look up the hierarchy, they see you first.

128. Never pass the opportunity to give a man a compliment.

Although this may sound like a shallow suggestion, it is actually a tactic for bringing a woman's leadership strength of building relationships to the workplace.

We might hesitate to compliment a man at work because our training tells us that it does not belong there. Too motherly. Or not business-like.

But think about it. It opens up the communication culture to being about performance and assets that are worth noting.

In the information age, business is about building connections and relationships.

When was the last time someone passed on a compliment to you? Felt good, huh? So pay it forward. This goes for women too, but we are more generous in doling out compliments to other women. Men need positive reinforcement too, and should not be only compliments about handsome attire. Look for something that he has handled well lately. A tough decision or a dicey situation with a customer.

And oh, don't expect him to take it graciously. Although he may, it could be that you disarmed him enough with your charm that he is speechless. Good one...

129. Let people pull in front of you when you are stopped in traffic on the way to work. It will set your tone for the day.

130. Park the farthest away from the building and walk.

Keep a pair of comfortable shoes with you if needed.

131. Consider what you stand for as a woman in leadership. Work at a job that is in accord with that.

132. Don't look at your job as a race between genders.

There is a danger in discussing gender issues. In essence we are calling attention to it.

Truthfully, it is unavoidable not to recognize certain differences between men and women, but do not go so far as to make it a discussion about "them and us." Instead we should feel comfortable understanding and embracing gender tendencies, as well as individual skills.

For a workplace to appreciate the talents of both men and women they must stop avoiding the conversation about gender dissimilarities. We are adamant that both have great talents and abilities to bring to the workplace.

133. Consider what would happen if you just ignore the bad stuff.

134. See your job as an investment in your future. Do it for you.

135. Donate a few hours to a local classroom, visiting them or letting them tour your space. Teach them about your business.

As a wholly balanced leader, your responsibilities include consideration of the community around you. Contribute to the world outside your business walls.

136. Develop your employees through constant training. Find out how you can support what they are learning.

You may have set a goal for yourself to be a lifelong learner. Others may strive for the same. If you are in a position to facilitate the development of others, see it as an honor.

137. Send your employees to self-improvement or skill-building classes.

Get to know their developmental goals so that you can encourage them.

138. Ignore your phone when someone is in your office.

139. Stand when a guest enters your office.

140. Never hit "Reply All" on an email that may incriminate someone or may be interpreted as critical.

141. Handle sensitive matters face-to-face, never electronically.

142. Use efficiency in your emails. Write a summary at the top so that the reader gets a quick understanding of the entire message.

143. Rarely use the high priority flag in emails. It is seen as overreacting.

We could go on and on about emails and other emerging electronic doodads. These four tips are the ones we thought may be most often violated and needed reminding.

144. It's okay to hug in business.

I love and appreciate that we can do this.

See how many advantages we have? Men do not really have this as an option ... well, kind of. ...

And when you are greeting someone with a hug, let him be the first to let go.

145. Accept help from others and use them as allies.

Men do this all the time. They see others as allies in getting what they need and will not hesitate to use them.

146. Do not tolerate sloppiness in your employees.

147. Keep a daily journal on your employees so that you can be fair at annual reviews.

Good leadership reviews need to have a more objective field of performance from which to draw. A journal dedicated to jotting down observations about your employees is an effective way to keep your judgment from being limited to only what you can remember.

When appraisals come along, you will want it to be a formality, not feedback you have to suddenly come up with. If you simply recall what that employee has done over the past 6-months, you fall prey to what is called the "recency effect," remembering what comes to mind which is likely the most recent behavior.

148. Be an optimist about people's potential for talent.

149. Surround yourself with smart men and women.

We become easily influenced by the company we keep. Look at the five people who work closest with you. Do they bring about better results in you? Do you learn from them?

150. Be proud.

People will respond to you based on clues that they see in the way you act.

If you send a message of insecurity, they will be hesitant to follow. If you show shyness, they will not expect you to conquer barriers. If you behave as if a woman is a second-class citizen, they will treat you as such.

Think about what you have to be proud of.

151. Be teachable.

Did you used to think you knew it all?

152. Good approaches to being a great leader are easy to find. Don't tour the world looking for the best. Find a decent, simple one and live by it.

153. When defining yourself as a female leader, think about what you mother used to tell you: *be yourself.*

Know yourself – easily said.

Time for introspection is absolutely critical for every woman in a position of influence. What are your ideals? What are your needs? Where did those stem from? Are they uniquely yours? Or have some been defined by others, such as an overbearing parent or a demanding boss?

Once your voice becomes your own, your identity will unleash. Energy and confidence builds.

154. Look at your leadership trek as a story, with various chapters, some challenging, some triumphant.

Ever written your leadership story?

For many women, it is not limited to workplace experiences, but weaves in lessons learned in all aspects of their lives, including challenges, victorious events, and sudden left turns.

We all have an interesting background. Try relating yours to someone and see what comes out.

155. Define a personal development roadmap for your leadership track as a woman. Select a few stretch targets but keep the overall plan very manageable and balanced.

Begin with a list of your strengths. Identify how to best leverage those.

At some point, consider what your desired future holds for you and set a stake in the ground as to when to achieve it. By acknowledging intention and focus, you are likely to see results.

156. Use a confidant in the HR or training department or hire a coach to support your development plan.

157. Limit your use of absolutes in your daily language, such as "always," "everyone," "everyone," and "totally." It sounds amateurish.

158. Avoid using inflamed and judgmental words, such as "lazy" or "uncaring."

159. Speak in terms of fact, rather than inference.

Here you have three quick fixes for effectively leading through communications.

As a leader, your communications are amplified simply because of your position power. Avoid exaggerations and judgmental statements. When you use the absolutes, your statement is probably not accurate and your message embellished.

When describing something, stick to irrefutable observations, such as "she has been late 8 of the last 10 days to work." When you begin translating it into an inference, such as "she does not care about her job anymore", you are passing along a judgment that may or may not be true, BUT it should not be broadcast.

160. Don't compare employees to each other. It could quickly be interpreted as favoritism.

161. Do not whine. EVER.

It might be a fine line, but tone of voice can get you a long way and whining will get you nowhere.

People tune out whining quite quickly. Often there is something constructive in the middle of the moaning, so too bad it is lost in the complaining.

162. Teach your employees how to translate problems into opportunities for improvement, not as whining or complaining.

Senior leaders get weary of hearing grumbles, especially when emotion is attached to them. Instead of passing the negatives up the ladder, position issues as a business case for change.

Teach employees to translate their issues into statements that outline the problem and underline the cost to productivity. Have them report the problems without emotion, along with possible costs and solutions.

163. Cut out newsletter articles or announcements about your co-workers give it to them.

164. Don't point at someone when talking to him.

We sometimes misconstrue *control* for *command*. In an effort to maintain control, we drift into pushy without knowing it.

Watch for the signs, both verbal and non-verbal.

165. Change demands into questions. You will be surprised how responsive someone is when he can take part in the dialog.

166. When you are tempted to lose your temper, breathe deeply and visualize yourself as a cool chick.

Sure, use the word "chick." It'll make you feel more hip and maybe settle you down.

167. Don't ever use a toothpick in public.

Hopefully you do not need to be told this.

168. Envision yourself as a dynamic female leader.

Visualization is a powerful tool. Recent research is indicating that the brain cannot differentiate between what we actually experience and what we imagine. Visualization puts the neuropathways to work and supports your body in living what you desire to have happen.

So while we are at it here, expand the visualization to giving a successful speech, flawlessly leading a tough meeting, or interacting with your boss in a resounding way.

Next year, rule the world ...

169.   Keep yourself in shape. You will be more productive.

As a periodic exercise, highlight the key priorities in your life. The typical list includes areas like family, work, marriage, health, and spiritual direction.

Then let me push back on something – where does your physical health rank? Consider how many other areas are dependent on your health and well-being.

170. When hiring an outside contractor, consider the local guy and the integrity of the company, not the cheapest.

171. Resist being over-accommodating. You will quickly be labeled as a doormat.

172. Learn your administrative assistant's talents.

173. Learn what your administrative assistant expects of you.

Or for that matter, anyone that you heavily depend upon.

Understanding one another, knowing the full range of someone's capabilities, and appreciating what they expect of you are all critical building blocks of a strong working relationship.

This tip is an important one for maintaining important relationships in your life, and it is often easy to address.

174. When someone is angry, let him vent.

The technique of letting someone vent works when anyone is emotionally charged. For many men, it is necessary dumping that you will not want to interrupt.

Listen and empathize.

Then once the venting slows, be supportive in understanding its source, and lead the conversation to problem-solving.

175. Keep on top of the new electronic gadgets at the office and learn how to use them.

176. Be efficient at using your keyboard or take a class to learn.

It is not difficult to set yourself apart as a woman simply by gender.

Here is another way. Find an emerging technology -- something that seems trendy and people are talking about, then educate yourself about it. By being a little more informed about how to use it, you become a resource at the office and it lends credibility to your expertise.

At Skirt Strategies, we work with women of all generations, and frequently with those that have technical backgrounds. The advantage of those in the techie world is that they have such a natural aptitude for grasping new technologies. I love it!

The flip side, some women, often the baby boomer generation, that have not grown into their careers with the advantage of technical contraptions around them, and run the risk of looking incompetent around thingamajigs. Oh ma lord ... we have GOT to fix this. A 50-something woman can rapidly shrink into an inept image because of her technical failures.

If this is you, then these two tips are for you. Let's just change them from tips, into strong recommendations.

177. When tempted to criticize your boss, bite your tongue.

178. Never end a relationship by burning a bridge.

179. Learn to negotiate using your principles, not your emotion.

180. Model useful feedback methods.

181. Never get defensive when getting feedback and teach your employees this skill.

A healthy workplace uses ongoing feedback, both corrective as well as reinforcing (a nice way of saying negative and positive). Feedback should be informal as well as formal, on-the-spot, timely, descriptive, sent with care and thought, and supportive.

When feedback has these characteristics, it becomes a part of the culture and employees do not resist it. It should be welcomed as an insight for how to improve. With that, the recipient is less likely to become defensive.

182. Keep communicating the big picture to your employees.

Many women are good at keeping sight of the big picture. We can keep perspective while still seeing necessary tactics for progress. This is a great leadership asset.

Understanding your function in your business can be naturally motivational. A sense of purpose leads to self-worth.

The corollary of this: keeping others motivated by purpose.

The benefit of everyone working to make the overall objective happen: an augmented desire to interact with other departments. Terrific!

183. Spend time defining your personal values. Dig deep for what moves you, not what you *think* should move you or what you think someone else wants for you.

Here's some blank space. (hint hint)

184. Approach a challenging issue as you would a project.

This can be a helpful hint for those tasks that seem daunting or insurmountable.

Looking at an issue as if it were a project can light the pathway for resolving it. Instead of it being a big hairy problem, give it a life with a beginning and a wrap-up, so that you can visualize it being put to rest.

To do this, articulate a concise desired outcome. Then list what you presently know about the issue and what you do not know. Identify what may be in your way and make plans to abate those. Set some stakes in the ground for whittling away at the problem in pieces and then have the patience to plod through it unyielding.

Refer back to Tip #63 for a methodology on ways to approach this.

185. Lead in such a way that when your employees describe you behind your back, they describe you as someone who leads with consistent and high standards.

186. Don't get in a panic over a backlog of work. Chances are your job is designed for some backlog.

187. Reward good ideas.

188. Stay away from giving financial rewards.

Something we have learned in working with hundreds of various organizations - When it is about money, it becomes an activity about keeping it fair rather than making it a true reward.

Find rewards that are not tied to money.

189. Buy the colored paper clips.

190. Regularly tune up your fundamental skills.

Too many leaders forget this! Remember the bedrock of your skills, those that oil the entire machine.

Communication, conflict management, and goal-setting are all terrific skills that fade if they do not get practice and refining.

Skirt Strategies is filled with those.

Many women look at simple skills and scoff, stating that they are too basic and they are beyond needing these. Hey we gotta disagree!

Basics are building blocks to make everything else work. I have seen too many leaders get wooed into a complex leadership model thinking it was the hot new thing, yet their fundamental capabilities lacked. The Top Leadership Pantry Model for Composite Success won't work if you can't function as a leader. (don't look that Model up – I completely invented it)

191. When communicating, get to the heart of your message.

Say things in fewer words than you think you need. Men prefer not to deal with jabber, and if a woman rattles on, we get quickly labeled as Chatty Cathy's. I appreciate our need to use *talk* for interacting, but we too often overuse it.

Same goes for your writing skills. Review what you have written. By eliminating words, see how *few* it takes to say the same thing.

There is this exercise that we used to do in English class in college. It always amazed me. Take any paragraph you may write, such as an email. Now go through it with the objective of eliminating as many words as you can and still maintaining the meaning of the message. You will find that you can eliminate about 20% of the words. This little drill illustrates for you the extra fluff we use in our communications.

See the next page for some examples.

KATIE K. SNAPP and CAROL M. WIGHT

Example:

Change	To
a great number of times	often
during the course of	during
due to the fact that	because
I am in the receipt of	I have

192. Patronize the parking lot food van.

Help out the little guy in the Roach Coach.

193. Keep your radar up for how to improve.
The best teams know how to self-correct.

There's this silly story about a boiled frog that we consultants like to tell. It goes like this:

If you drop a frog into a pot of boiling water, know what he does? Well, he jumps out of course. But if you drop the frog into a pot of tepid water, then slowly turn the heat up so that the water eventually reaches boiling, he actually boils to death. ... frog legs for dinner.

This applies to humans in a business environment as well (but not the eating them for dinner part). Things change around us in such small increments that we don't notice. Yeah – we kinda get boiled eventually. Teams experience this when working together if they do not periodically assess their effectiveness.

One characteristic of a high-performing team that can be replicated is self-correction. A great team assesses itself recurrently and checks for complacency. They set goals on the fly and see that they adjust as needed.

194. Never underestimate the power of a well-tuned team.

Huge payoff potential.

The concept of teaming is proven. Every last leader should be incorporating at least a few teaming techniques or going the distance to achieve a high-performing team. Think useful tools such as problem-solving together, conflict management, clear communications, and action through decision-making.

Women are natural teambuilders because our private lives require pulling together varied resources for nurturing families and constructing communities. We are GREAT at this.

Your one caution, however, is not to begin using teaming as an organizational methodology without giving your employees training to learn teambuilding concepts! Doing that turns TEAM into a 4-letter word. Why? Because they hear from you how great teaming is and how much they will benefit from it, yet don't experience all that. They get tossed into it without knowing what to look for or how to take advantage of group dynamics.

A woman's natural tendency for collaboration is a strong beacon for a team. Use your talent here to help provide some of that training the team will need. Ergo, our next tip ....

195. Teach your employees the fundamentals of teamwork.

196. Develop a team name for your employee team. Identity breeds pride.

This is a simple little trick, and it works well. When a team has a name, it develops an identity, which aids in building uniqueness. It is then more likely to take on a life of its own rather than floundering into a death spiral.

Bonus: The process of naming a team can in itself be a team-building event.

197. Expand your vocabulary by learning a new word at least once a month.

A leader should be educated. So ya better SOUND educated.

198. Find three Italian words that you think sound beautiful. Use them in everyday language.

Must be said with flair:

Bella	beautiful
Matto	mad, insane
Gustare	to enjoy or relish
Maestro	expert
Lavoro	work
Un momento	a moment
Clientela	customers
Dolce	sweet, pleasant
Formaggio	cheese
Capisce?	Understand?
Molte grazie!	Many thanks!
A presto.	See you soon.

199. Listen intently to yourself as you speak. When you do, you will improve your clarity immediately.

So here's a quick fix for getting the communication skill refined without spending too much time. I call it the 2-channel method.

The conversation you are having in your head may be different than what is coming out of your mouth, especially if you are a little *loca*, but we won't go into that.

Perhaps you can think more quickly than your voice can process it into words. Nonetheless, it's coming out.

The skill involves increased awareness in listening to what is going on in your head. Carefully formulate what you want to say, and then articulate it in clear statements. Simpler is better. At the same time, tune an ear into what is coming out the mouth. This sounds like a juggling act of confused multitasking, but it can be done. (Or just use a recorder)

Like many skills, half the battle is in remembering to look for the approach and practicing it.

200. Learn to use the built-in thesaurus on your computer.

Before:

"Your last report looked like it needed help."

After:

"That recent report reflected deficiencies."

Maybe more stodgy than you'd like? Well, fine. Then use the thesaurus when you need a descriptive word or a better one than you have.

In your word processor, you can highlight the word, then right-click, select thesaurus. Voilà. aka Hey presto.

201. Start gathering personal stories that will define your leadership as a great female boss. Become a story-teller.

I used to carry a small spiral to capture these, but now I use the yellow stickies application in my iPhone. My best stories come from evenings with friends around a glass of wine, reciting our latest drama at work or a funny incident.

Capture those! They tell the story of who you are and what you have endured.

As you look back through your inventory of experiences, you will see patterns and habits. These brief flashes of your life narrate who you are.

Also, they will come in handy when you are looking for anecdotes in your next public speech.

202. Regularly ask your employees what you can do to make them more effective.

Indeed this could apply to anyone that you work with, not just employees. As a periodic exercise, I check into how effective people are around me and whether anything that I could do may augment their effectiveness. Sometimes I have resources they could use.

203. Compliment three employees every day.

You guessed it. These tips include men.

204. Act confident. When you do, people will treat you as a confident woman. That results in you feeling more confident.

This is referred to as the "fake it to make it" technique, and it truly works. It becomes a self-fulfilling prophesy, and takes a little practice and faith in yourself.

205. Remember that many leaders are often in situations where they have no clue what to do. A woman leader is no different. Don't ever show a lack of confidence.

206. Hold on to your good ideas, despite what others may say.

207. Listen to yourself during the next meeting and see how many times you criticize, and how many times you praise.

I dedicate this leadership tip to Debbie Downer.

208. When tempted to criticize someone, assume he (or she) has had a worse day than you.

209. Whistle a song from the 1970's and see who recognizes it.

I recommend the Doobie Brothers or Earth, Wind, and Fire.

There is absolutely no reason to do this other than to flesh out any fellow baby boomers.

And if you are a gen-x or gen-y, please adapt accordingly. Maybe OAR or Jason Mraz.

210. If you cannot read enough leadership books, subscribe to a summary service and read the executive summary.

Leadership books stimulate ideas and keep you sharp. Don't feel overwhelmed to take on all their recommendations (and yes I hear the irony in that), but instead to use them as a compass for learning what is going on out there.

Too many business books are contrived as the magic potion to solve all your problems and to see the world in a new way, yet I rarely read something *that* innovative.

Nonetheless, they get my creativity going and I find myself jotting down ideas and new approaches that I would not have otherwise discovered.

If you are not a whiz-bang reader, try subscribing to an audio club. Using a different learning method, listening instead of visual scanning, can stimulate you in a completely different way.

211. Set aside personal productivity time twice a week for no interruptions. As far as others know, you are off-site and unavailable.

It's a eureka! Why can your doctor insist that you sit in his office for an appointment without cell phones or other interruptions, but you cannot do it for yourself occasionally?

Not to be rude but ...

If you do not protect your time, no one will. Sure a little chatting here and there is tolerable, but know where you will be drawing the line. Educate your employees on where that line rests.

Teach your co-workers that an open door means you welcome them in, but you would like to avoid small-talk

Create a guarded timeslot that you label PPT - Personal Productivity Time. Treat it as you would vacation, or a critical meeting with a key client. Use this time for tasks needing your full attention as well as those that you would categorize as important.

With these tasks getting the attention they need, you will be remarkably more present and less distracted during the remainder of your day.

212. Gain new customers, but maintain the old. Keeping a present customer happy is more important than chasing after new ones.

This is a great reminder, and perhaps a pep-talk for the importance of the existing customer. They may be old news to you. Do you find it not so enamoring to keep them happy so you put efforts into the excitement of reaping new customers? This can be dangerous. You may eventually get the reputation for not providing good customer service, then your prospects for new business will be affected.

If this happens to you, you may ask yourself why your effort in retaining clients is losing your attention. It may be as simple as running out of ideas for retaining them. Or you are hesitant to ask how to make your service better because you are afraid of the answer.

For those of you with customer and other dependent relationships, spend a few minutes assessing where you are on this and whether you may be at risk of losing customers.

Consider throwing a customer appreciation party or giving existing customers a sweet deal on their next purchase.

213. Don't roll your eyes when considering an idea.

If you have a face that gives away emotion, learn to control it.

A client posed an idea to me once and then stated, "you are looking at me like I am growing a third-eye out of my forehead." We both laughed and I still smile at the way he just announced it to me so openly.

A not-so-positive incident also occurred when I once looked up at the ceiling to ponder a discussion in a staff meeting. The boss and I were not on good terms at that time and he jumped on me, accusing me of rolling my eyes. It was clearly not my intent, but no matter. Damage done.

Subconscious non-verbals or other poorly timed statements about others will taint your professional image.

214. Learn to empathize and to acknowledge others' situations. It is a major element of a great listener.

Empathy is one of a variety of skills that women deploy more readily than men. It is no wonder. We are wired to support families and raise children, requiring that we sense what goes on in others so that we can nurture survival.

It used to be that the skill of empathy was hard-pressed to find a place in a working environment. Productivity, transactional tasks, and command and control cultures would not support time spent on reflecting on how someone feels at work.

But today, nearly all of our industries, whether technical, educational, financial, or utilities are about the *people* as the most valued commodity. Instead of being told "you are not paid to think," we are asked "what do you think?" The business world is largely about interacting intellectually and being innovative around results.

Empathy is a powerful tool for drawing on people's ideas and turning around their participation by reflecting what they are experiencing emotionally. Responding to emotions by acknowledging them can keep them from being a barrier in forward progress, especially in a team situation. Empathy in action can run the range of a simple statement to reflect what someone said about not liking the time the meeting was set, to asking them to articulate their opinion about what is holding them back.

For the moms in the crowd - if you have ever been accused of having eyes in the back of your head, then you are great at sensing! You are likely a natural for empathy. Use it, grasshoppa.

215. Be genuine when building relationships.
People sense falseness.

This is a slam dunk for women because so many of us have inherent social skills. We like connecting to others in a personal, non-business way.

We also see others in the workplace with social equity, versus where they are in the hierarchy of the company.

And to give this some emphasis as to its importance, consider how men build relationships at work. They use that "good ol' boys' network."

Both genders link to those with whom we have the most in common. If the heirarchy in your organization is predominantly men, then your leadership is more likely to relate to men before they relate to you. This puts women at a disadvantage for moving into leadership ranks. We aren't seen as fitting in and we do not naturally fit into their "good ol' boys' network."

This requires that you move your relationship-building skill into high gear. Use your comfortable interpersonal skills for connecting and find genuine ways to relate to men at all levels.

216. Keep one fruitcake at work and see how many years it gets passed around.

217. Spice up the little things. Drop mandarin orange slices in your club soda.

218. Never talk about someone as soon as he leaves the room. It looks disrespectful, regardless of what you are saying.

I wish people could just read my mind when I was talking about someone and know that I *meant* it in the best way. Blah blah blah. But as women we get nailed immediately for being in attack mode, criticizing and gossiping, or it looks like we didn't have the courage earlier when the comment would have been to his face. I hate that, but I also understand where it comes from.

Just play it safe and be careful about what you say. You can often stay out of trouble by discussing situations, not *who* people are or what their value system is. Be diplomatic.

219. Use logic to sell an idea.

220. Use sentiment to build a relationship.

One of the reasons men are good at negotiating is that they leave the emotion out of it. When they get a rejection, they can let it roll off their backs. This keeps their mind clear and unaffected to forge forward with a counter-offer.

Women, however, often walk into negotiations and immediately set ourselves up for failure by apologizing for "having to ask" or saying "I know this is probably not a good time."

A day in the life of a leader is filled with efforts to influence others and to gain buy-in. Hesitating in your language or using emotion as the lever rarely works, yet women believe that since they "feel" something, then it must be the reason for getting others to do it.

Wrong. Having a strong urge or emotion for wanting something should not lead you to use that for justification. However, it should lead you to dig into that emotion to ask yourself *why* you are feeling it.

221. When you need to use a negative word, find a foreign language equivalent.

"Verboten" is more appealing than "forbidden." It makes you sound worldly and it takes the edge off the negativity.

Italian	Accidenti!	Oh crap
	Stupido	Stupid
Spanish	Vámonos	Let's go
Russian	Nyet	No
French	Zut	Damn
	Bouge toi	Move it!
German	Verboten	Forbidden
	Achtung!	Caution!

Uber in front of anything
Super or over, as in uber-geek
Handschuhschneeballwerfer
Coward
(extra points for using that one)

In a pinch, just add a foreign accent of your choosing to your everyday English. That *might* work, or it may make you look like an uber-fool.

222. Know how to balance operating by the numbers with operating by your gut.

223. Know how to balance trusting people with looking over their shoulders.

224. Know how to balance your customers' needs with your company's needs.

I call these last three the daily dilemmas. They are choices that you must make every day. How cognizant are you about choosing yours? These little moments of truth define who you are as a leader. We call these work-work balance.

Exercise: Periodically assess where you stand on remaining balanced. Ask yourself about one of the areas in the list of three above.

225. Find a way of connecting to others at your workplace by discovering commonalities about their situations and their backgrounds.

Be careful when socializing with your subordinates that they do not abuse your authority with their familiarity.

Trust is more readily built when people have something in common. And THAT is why socializing with your co-workers is so beneficial.

226. Be strong in admitting a weakness. It builds trust.

It takes strength to admit a weakness. Not only will it show your backbone, but it will also disclose vulnerability. This is a major step toward achieving trust with others – revealing something personal about you.

Could you overdo this one? Maybe.

My guess is that you will know it if you spend too much time talking about your blunders. If that seems to be the case, take inventory of where you stand on your mistakes and map out a plan that will bring you a near-term success, something that will get you back on the horse quickly.

227. Learn to delegate the decision-making
process.

Someone comes into your office, and asks
"What should I do about blah blah, etc.?" Now,
practice this with me – you say "I trust you to
make that decision."

Did that hurt so much?

228. Demonstrate efficiency by managing your time well.

The flashy electronic gadgets that control your life may also deprive you of managing your schedule so well. Use the techniques that best work for you, regardless of the trends.

Sometimes the handy TO-DO list on a hand-written post-it note is the most successful.

229.   Recognize activities that appear
important simply because they are urgent.

Stephen Covey has built a model around this that maps the *important v urgent*. We naturally respond to urgent issues, but often it is simply because they are *urgent*. What about being important?

As an example, your phone rings during a family dinner. Our first reaction is to jump up, see who it is, and possibly answer it. But what could be more important than family time together? Why would we even consider interrupting it for an unknown?

While we are on the subject of interruptions, improve your time management by taking an inventory of what your interruptions look like during the day. If you were to build a list of those items that interrupted your attention, where would they fall in priority?

Most of us tend to fall into one of two categories with email as a constant urgency. If you are in that enviable category of not being slave to the incoming emails, then consider turning the "ding" off or closing your mail program completely. Set a time on your calendar to exclusively work emails. Don't fall into the trap of thinking a new email needs immediate attention.

For those of you that simply cannot afford to ignore emails throughout the day, then clarifying the *important* in your life is critical before all those *urgent*'s start ruling you.

The learning philosophy at Skirt Strategies is built upon this need to set intent and focus, without all the noise of the *urgent*.

230. Keep track of your employee's talents and find a way to occasionally use them.

231. Find out which instruments your employees can play. You'll be surprised how easily you can put together a "band".

It can be so surprising how many people have these secret lives with secret talents.

The hiding-out must stop! Drag them into the limelight.

This can be especially useful just before the annual Holiday party. Hee hee, devious.

232. Keep a first aid kit in your desk.

Really ... it helps to have a central location for the (dare I say it) emergency tampon. You'll be a hero.

233. Learn what is important to your boss.

234. Let your boss know what is important to you.

235. Find something to learn from your boss.

More about relationship building. If it is not obvious to you by now, the key is learning about the values, perspectives, and priorities of others.

Take this on as a challenge for your personal growth. Find some dedicated time to spend with him or her discussing his viewpoints on business issues and his outlook for the company.

236. Think strategically. Work tactically. Align the two.

Women are skillful big picture thinkers. It could be that this keeps you from considering the detailed execution of tasks.

So ask yourself if you do both well, then consider how you may better balance it. A gifted leader has good skillsets in both the strategic as well as the tactical arenas. If she does not, then she is adept at recognizing the need to delegate, as well as surrounding herself with people who can pick up the slack.

237. Be careful what you say in public. The next table my have big ears.

If you have been burned by this, you are likely not to repeat the error.

And if you have been in the position where you were talking about something that, if overheard, would be disastrous, then I might ask you whether it was a necessary conversation. Could be that it was, but be careful. Needing to hold your voice down could indicate that it is something you should not be sharing anyway.

238. Find a key spot to sit at during meetings where you can hear and be heard. Never hide in the back.

Little things send a strong message.

There is a tendency for many women to give men the seat at the table. Ever noticed that men don't really do that for us? So many drivers affect this behavior.

For one, we live our lives as natural nurturers, which gives us a servitude mindset. We see ourselves as the backroom enablers for others to be successful – an important role, for sure, but one that gets reflected to others as "I see myself as unimportant."

We also, may give up our seats in our quest to protect male egos, knowing that it is not as critical for us to take the front and center as it may be for someone with a fragile ego.

It could also be that you are feeling you won't be listened to anyway, so why push your way into the front row? This stems from your own self-confidence issues.

Resist the urge to fall prey to any of these de-motivations. Sit at the table. If this is *your* meeting, sit at the head of the table.

239. Find another department in the company that you need to work with better. Make it a project to improve the relationship.

It is not uncommon for parts of the company to work *against* other parts. Some competitive behavior is valuable, but you rarely want it internally.

The competition stems from several roots. Some of it is simply our demeanor as Americans. We cannot resist fighting to be the top dog. (there's a joke in there about the female dog, but let's not go there)

But the most common cause of win-lose behaviors within a company is a lack of cooperation at higher levels. The tone is set when upper levels hold firmly to their turfs as if they are in a race to see who can accomplish more.

At all levels, companies are rarely spending time understanding the function of other areas of the business, and that breeds a naïveté about the power of collaborating.

A little relationship building begins with some understanding. The effort will be worth the time invested.

240. Keep confidences when your employees open up to you.

241. Learn when to bite your tongue.

242. Learn when to intervene.

243. Learn when to let someone struggle.

There's a guy named Kenny, and he says "Know when to hold 'em. Know when to fold 'em." That's kinda related. Maybe?

> **244.** Work with your company to conduct periodic emergency drills so that everyone knows what to do in an emergency.

It seems a little silly, but it is another opportunity for you to utilize your leadership skills.

It is also just a good idea for keeping the workplace a little safer.

And if, perhaps, you are a woman in the position of trying to build others' confidence in you as a leader, especially an emerging one, then something like this is recommended. It shows initiative.

245. At the end of each day, make a list of your next day's tasks. You will go home calmer and sleep better.

Many of us get stressed over feeling that our workloads are out of control. Yet, have you ever noticed that when you look at a list of everything you need to get done tomorrow, it packages it up into a manageable little bundle?

One trick we recommend is to mentally streamline the tasks and their intensities. See also if you can put them into a small, simple list. Then be an optimist. For those pessimists in the crowd, pretend you're an optimist for a moment.

If this works for you, then your workload stress may be caused by feeling that you are losing control of defining your to-do list, not necessarily getting it accomplished.

Then in the morning, take a deep breath, and remind yourself that it is possible to get it all accomplished.

By the way, every once in a while I use the "so what if I fail to get it all done" mentality. What the heck? Who cares? It just works for me!

246. Manage your emotion by understanding how your environment influences you.

Well, true, but much of it is a reflection of how you are seeing it. What conditions create a pleasant feeling for you and which ones just torque you off?

How you react to your environment is YOUR CHOICE. You may not be able to affect your world, but you have complete control in how you react to it. Ja?

So, learn tricks for lifting your mood. Put on the iPod headphones. Read a mindless magazine. Stand by a playground and watch kids be creative. Bury your toes in a soft rug. Take a valium. **

** Skirt Strategies does not advocate, promote, or march the streets to campaign for the use of narcotics, or other mood-changing drugs. ...unless you consider a smooth Cabernet a drug, then never mind.

247. Smile when you are on the phone. The other person can hear it.

This really is true. (Can you tell I am smiling as I write this?)

248. Buy the Starbuck's for the person in the drive-thru behind you.

Every so often I do something like this and I beam for the rest of the afternoon.

I am a believer in karma. Maybe it's just that when people put positive energy into the universe, it perpetuates positive energy and creates a feeling of satisfaction.

But as a scientist, I look at it like this: when we take our power of influencing others and translate it into affirmative activities, it increases the amount of that upbeat energy out there. Only good can come from that. The more, the better. And sooner or later I will be the recipient of some.

249. Strive to be someone's role model.

KATIE K. SNAPP and CAROL M. WIGHT

ACKNOWLEDGEMENTS

I, Katie, so appreciate Carol for helping me with this book and would like to acknowledge her. I am sure she would like to do the same for moi.

Dittos ... from Carol.

ABOUT SKIRT STRATEGIES

At Skirt Strategies we empower high potential women to lead and succeed.

We guide professionals to gracefully move into positions of leadership, giving women clarity of purpose that drives their productivity. Through our monthly membership, they connect with like-minded women and receive videos, blogs and tele-classes that help them communicate their authority with self-confidence, nurture their natural leadership skills, and uncover a distinctive professional style that gets women noticed and heard.

KATIE K. SNAPP and CAROL M. WIGHT

`

Made in the USA
Charleston, SC
10 January 2013